The
Healing
Garden

"How I Healed Myself"

Written by

Patricia Majka,
CRDH, BASDH

ABOUT THE AUTHOR

Patricia Majka, CRDH, BASDH, has been writing poetry for over 30 years and found a love and passion for this talent as early as senior high school. Her first poem was published in her high school's poetry book and earned her a superior grade in her writing course. After entering a college English course, her enthusiasm and creativity for writing poetry were ignited and sparked the creation of Patricia Poetry. Her company presents a consumer with a unique experience, for those who would like special words written for special people, delivered as a *"bouquet of word flowers".* For more information on Patricia and her unique talents, please visit her website www. patriciapoetry.com.

DEDICATION

This book of poetry is dedicated to all of the people who have loved and supported me throughout my life. I am only as *good* as the people I surround myself with. I begin by dedicating this book to the one I call my "guardian angel", the ONE, who has truly loved me unconditionally, supported me both mentally and financially, and has given me the courage to enter college as a mature adult, follow my dreams and most importantly, do what makes me truly happy. He always says, "Go For It", and I have done just that. Being happy with oneself is more important than physical things. It took me half of a lifetime to grasp that simple concept. To my children, Lauren and Mason, having the two of you has been the most gratifying experience in life. I love you both and am proud of everything you have accomplished. To my sister Cyndy, you have been a source of inspiration to write poetry of healing. I love you. To my best friends, Vickie, Cristina, Trista, Maria, Carol, Kathy, Therese, Hannah, Denise, Sonya, and Mirian, I love all of you and thank you for your love and support throughout my life. I wouldn't be where I am today without each of you. To my two mamas, Mama Carol and Madre Sharon, you were there when my own mother couldn't be. You both have loved me as your own and have shown me love when I needed it the most. The affection I have for you can be unmatched and the care you have given as mothers is immeasurable. I thank you both from the bottom of my heart.

"How I Healed Myself"

It was upon my resignation,
When I found myself alone…
That I learned appreciation,
To believe in the unknown.

I had one sure thing to count on,
As I looked deep inside myself…
To draw faith and inspiration,
That had been put upon a shelf.

The Healing Garden is a place,
Where I can always go…
Where sunshine's on my face,
While the trickling waters flow.

Spend hours there and meditate,
To clear my busy mind…
It's there I do not hesitate,
For clarity comes in time.

The years I've spent searching for peace,
I thought would never come…
But all the while, was in my reach,
For I knew he was the one.

The one on whom I could depend,
When I felt helpless and alone…
My savior, until life's end,
My intentions, he had known.

And after many hours,
Spent in my happy place…
The feelings of ache and sadness,
Have forever been replaced.

With gratitude and love inside me,
That erases all that pain…
Took away all the anxiety,
Now my healed heart remains…

Patricia
POETRY

4

A Moment in Time

What's in your heart is what matters most,
It's all about what's inside…
While yesterday's dreams seem like a ghost,
It's for all of us to decide.

When we truly really think about,
The life we've all been given…
Whether we live with, or live without,
It's a temporary living condition.

Material things don't matter much,
It's the love of family and friends…
The ones we cannot physically touch,
Is what matters in the end.

Look at this moment in our lives,
On a momentary scale…
For some time soon, we will see the light,
And we'll know we all prevailed.

Written by Patricia Majka

Patricia

POETRY

Beauty

The fresh cut flowers,
The grass, the sky…
It's all so beautiful,
We ask ourselves why?

How can this beauty,
Be all around us…
There has to be a reason,
A why, a must.

There's only one answer,
To the question at hand…
God created this beauty,
With his master plan.

To give us our peace,
Through shedding his blood…
And showing his grace,
And the power of his love.

We are all blessed,
In one way or another…
Our journey begins,
With our father and mother.

From then our lives are,
Whatever we make it…
And the chances we take,
There's no way to fake it.

Just trust in our Lord,
And the grace of his love…
And God's blessing will reign,
Upon you from above.

Calm

It's time to be calm,
And reflect on how we…
As a people, a nation,
Have learned how to be.

Be thankful for family,
And all our good friends…
For that's how it should be,
In time we will mend.

And someday we'll look back,
And we'll truly see…
Our country was attacked,
By an unseen enemy.

But what it has taught us,
As a nation you see…
We all made such a fuss,
But it was a blessing to me.

We've gained time with loved ones,
As the whole world has stopped…
Took the time to slow down,
Look how we'd been robbed.

Of the peace and tranquility,
That this rat race takes…
Away from our ability,
To see what's right in our face.

This newfound reality,
That we've come to know…
Days pass with uncertainty,
But forward we'll go.

We have been blessed to be,
Safe and sound in our homes…
And we will remove fear,
As we joyfully overcome.

Written by
Patricia Majka

Patricia

Drifting Away

Like the driftwood lined,
Along a sandy shore…
The waves that washed it in,
Continue to eb and flow.

There is a natural beauty,
That we may not appreciate…
For the things in life,
That are truly great.

A boat ride can refresh your mind,
And wash your cares away…
Be present in the pretty sunshine,
And take some time to play.

So stop, reset, and make some space,
And truly look around you…
Let yourself be here and in this place,
There are things that will inspire you.

Like the wood I saw on the sandy shore,
And being with my special friends…
Who inspired me to write this poem,
I wish this day would never end!

Written by
Patricia Majka

God's glory

His glory weighs more,
Than what I'm going through…
His presence, can't be ignored,
I'm sure what his blessings can do.

For when I put him first,
He will guide my way with light…
And if I live unrehearsed,
He will always be in my sight.

For it's his purpose,
That makes mine complete…
My destiny lies soley in his hands,
In my heart, I don't compete.

For my blessings outweigh my burdens,
And god's grace eraces my shame…
His hope removes my hardships,
With the mere utterance of his name.

For I will forever cherish him,
In my heart, the only place…
Where he knows my relationship with him,
And the power of his mercy and his grace.

Written by:
Patricia Majka

Today is the First Day

Today is the first day,
Of the rest of my wonderful life…
I will always try to find a way,
To see it through clear eyes.

To know that everyone around me,
Loves and supports me in all that I do…
Will help me move forward,
And live happily and feel new.

As I wake up each morning,
And get out of my comfortable bed…
I will thank God for my blessings,
And my new life that lies ahead.

And if the day comes when I feel sad,
I will remind myself of this…
Instead of being angry and getting mad,
I will remember who wrote me this.

My sister, my friend, who loves me,
More than I could ever know…
She tells me and she shows me,
This poem is to help me grow.

Written with Love for my Sister Cyndy

Oh Brother...

Oh brother, my brother,
I've been afraid all my life…
I watched you hit my mother,
When you had a fight.

As a child growing up,
In a house full of pain…
With anger and violence,
The suffering was insane

I managed to heal from,
The illness and sadness…
And began to overcome,
Which turned into gladness.

Your actions have always been,
For you only, to own…
For how you have treated me,
And what you have shown.

So, don't you dare lecture me,
Or assume what I know
About addiction and dependency
Because I have my own.

To love and to care for her,
Is not enabling you see…
Because I am part of her
And she's part of me.

I've always been there for her,
Through the good and bad parts…
And what I do for her,
Comes straight from my heart.

I only reached out to you,
To open a door…
And let you inside,
Of our family's war.

To fight this addiction,
And make a new start…
But I can see now,
That it wasn't my part.

My Best Friend,
Vickie Vic

There is a time,
In all our lives…
When we must deal,
With stress and strife.

And some of us,
Have been given more…
And always must,
Try to endure.

I know that now,
It seems that you…
Really don't know,
What to do.

But always know that,
You can lean on me…
To be there for you,
In your time of need.

That's what a friend does,
Come night or day…
To be there and listen,
Along the way.

Sometimes our life,
Can be so hard…
For we don't know,
What's in the cards.

These tough bad times,
We must go thru…
To help us shine
And make us new.

I'll be beside you,
As your forever friend…
To pick you up,
And help you mend.

I love you Vic!

Patricia
POETRY

"Trigger"

It's lonely without you here old friend,
Just, the shear mention of your name…
Brings tears, to my eyes once again,
My life will never be the same.

You were bigger than life, and always by my side,
In our home, and with me at work…
Sitting by my desk, my big boy wide-eyed,
The mascot of my office, that's for sure.

When clients ask me where my "Trigger" is,
My answer is always hard to say…
I tell them he's passed over the Rainbow Bridge,
But his memory will forever stay.

Written in Loving Memory of Trigger for Joanna
By: Patricia Majka

Patricia
POETRY

The Pearl

What comes from an oyster,
And is loved by every girl…
A white gem full of glory,
For God gave us the pearl.

Love, generosity and purity,
Rare and worthy of our praise…
Can be worn by us as jewelry,
Almost every single day.

For some they have more meaning,
Then just a precious gem…
They represent a feeling,
That comes deep from within.

A gift of love and protection,
Some come in sets of three…
Created by God's Kingdom,
A symbol of love and integrity.

So wear your pearls and clearly,
Know that they were just bought…
By someone who loves you dearly,
You are always in his thoughts.

For my EPIK Friend, Sonya
Love,
Pat

Patricia
POETRY

"The One"

Life doesn't come with a hand-written plan,
But one thing is for sure, you were meant to be my man.

I don't know how, or where, or when or why?
I never imagined or thought I could even try…
To deserve the love of someone such as you,
My person, my soulmate, who made all of my dreams come true.

To GOD, I will be grateful, until I take my last breath,
For written in his master plan, is the reason why we met…
If there is one thing you should remember, and never ever forget,
You are my only love, the best I'll ever get.

You are the reason I live and breathe,
And the rising of the sun…
You're my now, my forever,
You'll always be "the one".

Dedicated to my person…
With all my love

Patricia

Growth

As I sit here this morning,
Looking over the lake…
I'm watching the water,
And the ripples it makes.

Like a wandering child,
Looking for a safe place…
I look in it's wild,
The reflection upon my face.

What I see is a woman,
Who once was a girl…
She is someone so strong now,
In this great big new world.

I have found faith,
A freedom to be…
A child full of grace,
And beauty you see.

Wherever my path decides to go,
There is one thing I want you to know…
Like the moving waters,
Don't know where they'll be,
I know that you'll always be right here with me.

Written by
Patricia Majka

Patricia
POETRY

"Shades of Pink"

Oh, just look at that sky,
Varying shade of pink…
We ask ourselves why,
And we begin to think.

How does the natural beauty,
Shine down from above…
The answer is absolutely,
Through his peace and his love.

So next time you look up,
And see deep shades of red…
Remember our Lord's love,
And the blood that he shed.

Through all of his mercy,
And his mighty grace…
He created that beauty,
To shine down on our face.

Patricia

POETRY

What I Love

Creating beauty through writing words,
Is something that I love to do…
They're expressions that can and will be heard,
By bringing joy as they are viewed.

As I write a meaningful greeting card,
I keep the sender's thoughts in mind…
As the receiver unexpectedly views the reward,
In the words that they will find.

The intention is always to spread true joy,
In our ever-changing world…
To send some love and fill a void,
In someone's heart and in their soul.

Written by
Patricia Majka

Teacher

A teacher is someone,
Who gives without taking…
By preparing a student,
A professional she is making.

The hours she pours,
Into everything she does…
Do not feel like chores,
She does it with love.

Grading, critiquing, analyzing and such,
Sometimes it may feel,
Like it's really all too much.

But just when it seems,
Like it's too much to bare…
Her student graduates,
And "makes it" out there.

For that is what you,
Have prepared us to do…
It takes a special person,
And that person is you.

Written by
Patricia Majka

Patricia

Perspective

Don't compare yourself to people
God created you to be…
Praised high upon a steeple,
You're not just likes on a news feed.

Stop scrolling for life's answers,
From strangers on a page…
As life it does not pamper,
The truth, it comes with age.

It's all in your perspective,
And how you look at things…
God's given you directive,
On how your life should be.

So looking back don't label,
Yourself as the victim…
Your strength will soon enable,
You just have to trust him.

And once you do surrender,
And live your life with faith…
Your anxiety will end I'm sure,
In God's hands your life does wait.

Written by Patricia Majka

Patricia
POETRY

"Anniversary"

Here we are nine years have passed,
Some people said it would never last…
In spite of their doubts we're still going strong,
For we always knew it would last this long.

A love like ours will never die,
The feelings we have are a natural high…
Today is the day it all started,
And we live each day never to be parted.

Written by
Patricia Majka

Patricia

"True Love"

Thankful, peaceful tranquil,
That's how I need to feel…
Anxious, nervous, uncertain,
Is the way I've come to be.

Working, running, stressed-out,
Is how I've always lived…
The only thing I've ever done,
Is give, give, give.

Someone loving me for me,
Is nothing I've ever known…
I'm so used to having to,
Make it on my own.

I want you to know that,
I listen to every word you say…
And I appreciate and love you,
More and more each day.

This life is a precious gift,
And I've been so very blessed…
To be lucky to be loved by you,
And experience true happiness.

You are truly one of a kind,
My love, my guardian angel…
And always in my mind,
And there for me without fail.

I love you today and tomorrow,
And all the rest of our days…
You've shown me how to love,
In oh so many ways.

The time that you've given me,
Is so meant to be…
I'll finally get to find out,
What it means to be me.

"The Fight"

Dedicated to the BLM Movement

The news, the news,
We seem to lose…
The fight, the fight,
We have the right.

The light, the light,
Do not lose sight…
The prize, the prize,
Is in our eyes.

The change, the change,
It's in our veins…
The blood, the blood,
No more flood.

Written by
Patricia Majka

Patricia

Strength

Written by
Patricia Majka

I found a new strength,
Way deep down in me…
A peace and a feeling,
I thought could not be.
It began back in March,
When I made a decision…
To changes life's trajectory,
At a moment's decision.
Slow down, take a breath,
Live a little bit…
It's something I've done,
With no lasting regrets.
For sometimes in life,
You're thrown a curve ball…
But now looking back,
I deserved it all.
But at the time,
I was filled with fright…
And with having faith,
I thought I just might.
Have the strength and the courage,
To just make it through…
And look to the future,
With a bright shiny view.
And when I look back,
I can really see…
That there never was doubt,
God had plans for me.

"The Beach"

The Beach is my happy place,
The sand's beneath my feet…
Warm breezes blowing on my face,
It's where I feel complete.

Warm sun shining down on me,
The beach is where I want to be.

So many memories as a child,
Playing in the surf…
My mind goes wild,
Whenever I get the urge.

To walk along the sea,
The beach is where I want to be.

It's a huge part of me,
It's where I come from…
In my future, I do see,
Myself lounging in the sun.

One day my dreams will become my reality,
The beach is where I'm going to be.
Where my new home, will be waiting for me.

Written by
Patricia Majka

Patricia

"Our Guardian Angels"

When you chose to take your oath to serve,
Who knew what that would mean…
For those you saved sure did deserve,
The chance to live disease free.

You're more than just a healthcare worker,
You're a hero to us all…
The sacrifices you made for sure,
So others would not fall.

We appreciate all that you have done,
To help this world in need…
I dedicate this poem to the one,
I hope everyone will read!

Dedicated to all of the Healthcare
Heroes during the 2020 Pandemic…
Thank you for that you've done
and continue to do!

Written by
Patricia Majka

Patricia

POETRY

Letting Go With Love

The hardest thing I've ever done,
Is to let you go from me…
But I think that it is the one
And only way you'll see.

That as much as I love you,
I also have to love myself…
And the things you say and do,
Have been destructive to my health.

I know I don't know what is in your soul,
And I don't want to say things to hurt you…
But when we last spoke, you cut me whole,
And at this point, I don't know what to do.

I think I've always been there for you;
In good times and in bad…
But now, it's different for me too,
I will miss the friendship we had.

The important thing from this point on,
Is for you to heal your heart…
You'll have your sponsor to count on,
As I can't play that part.

I hope that you will find some peace,
And comfort in your life…
And that it comes to you with ease,
And doesn't cause more strife.

The life we're given is a gift,
We must not take for granted…
So look inside and find that shift,
Remove the view that's slanted.

I wish you nothing but the best,
And pray for you every day…
And for your life, enjoy the rest,
I've said what I needed to say.

I love you and wish you nothing but the best and will think of you every day.

Written by
Patricia Majka

Patricia

What's Standing in your Way?

Do you wish you could be as strong as the trunk of a tree,
And do you feel like you are a weak and flimsy branch?
The difference in how you feel and what you truly see,
Comes from within you if you'd only take a chance.

For sometimes we don't see what we have inside of us,
We hide behind the fear that really isn't there…
It's easy to make excuses and refuse to ever discuss,
We don't take that chance and pretend that we don't care.

So what's it going to take to make you understand,
And to be thankful for what you have and learn to say…
Look beyond the fear you feel and finally take a stand,
Because *YOU* are what is standing in your way!

Written by
Patricia Majka

Patricia
POETRY

Poetry in Motion

At a very early age,
I already knew…
That writing my poetry,
Was something I'd do.

For the stories I conjured,
And made up in my head…
I thought, and I pondered,
Where I might be led.

I wrote my first poem,
At the age of fifteen…
It was one thing I'd known,
That was special to me.

I'd always been told,
That I had a great talent…
But as I grew old,
I became very gallant.

And then after taking,
Your college English course…
I began to start making,
A new career choice.

You sparked my desire,
For writing you see…
I'll sing to the choir,
You brought the best out in me.

As I graduate from college,
A grown woman whose changed…
With a newly found knowledge,
My whole life remains.

I've spent many hours,
Writing poetry, you see…
Sending Bouquets of Word Flowers
Through Patricia's Poetry.

Dedicated to all of my English Instructors,

In Recognition of National Poetry Month

April 2020

Patricia

Dentistry During a Pandemic

We, as dental professionals,
Practicing our craft every day…
Oh, the stories we could tell,
We have so much to say.

Our patients become our families,
Our practices, their dental homes…
We face so many adversities,
In many different time zones.

The "old" no longer works for us,
As we adapt to a "new" norm…
The way we used to practice,
Has taken on a new form.

The way you choose to look at this,
Is entirely up to you…
We know our patients need us,
So, we'll do what we have to do.

We will get thru this crisis,
Become stronger on the other side…
Our resilience oh so steadfast,
And *together*, we will rise!

Written by
Patricia Majka

Patricia
POETRY

My "Mama" Carol

From the time I was a little girl,
Beginning at the age of twelve…
I knew you'd be part of my world,
For you gave me so much of yourself.

I'd ride my bike up to your store,
And you would teach me so much…
About jewelry and love and many things more,
You had the sweetest touch.

I always knew I could count on,
You and Mike, to love me as…
The daughter you always wanted,
But the one you never had.

And as I grew up, you never forgot
To make sure that I was okay…
Those are the things I will never forget,
And remember them, to this day.

The love I have for you cannot,
Be said with a word or two…
But I hope you know,
That this poem was written,
To express all the love I feel for you.

With all my love,
Pat

Patricia

There's something you're missing,
because of your strife…
Our good Lord has given you,
a beautiful life.

Although you can't see it,
it's just under there…
Inside of your mindset,
it's there if you dare.

With one step then two steps,
then three and then four…
You've made the best choice yet,
the future is all yours.

I know it seems too hard,
and scary at times…
So brave is what you are,
and a hero of mine.

The time shall go very fast,
as you move ahead…
Time to undo the past,
and get out of your head.

You're going to feel better,
just you wait and see…
For along with this letter,
comes much love from me

I'll be thinking about you,
each night and each day…
And praying God keeps you,
safe in every way.

I love you my sister,
my very best friend…
Just know that I miss you,
with love, you will mend.

With all of my love,

Your sister,

PAT

"Everything will be Alright"

Sometimes we make choices,
That don't make any sense…
In our heads, we hear voices,
For which we'll have to make amends.

At this moment right now,
You are feeling very sad…
Thinking what you did and how,
And thinking that you are bad.

But always remember this,
As you go about your day…
My one and only wish,
Is for you to find your way.

You have the love and support,
Of your family and friends…
And so you won't resort,
To the way it's always been.

So, each and every morning,
As you begin your brand-new day…
It's time to start exploring,
Who you'll be and what you'll say.

Move away from how you used to be,
And look forward to your future…
Forget the past, you'll find security,
About the life you will incur.

For everyone feeling sadness in this time of insecurity, this was written for you!

Patricia

POETRY

To Thine Own Self Be True

Someone always told me,
The truth shall set you free..
But they don't live by that advice,
They live in fear of humiliation you see.

For to be one's authentic self,
You must be able to look into the mirror…
And who you see looking back at you,
Could not become any clearer.

For to live your life to show something,
That was never really true…
Would be a waste of life,
Because you were never really you.

Passion, Pleasure, Prophet

When you have a desire to do something, it's called a passion.

When that desire overwhelms you with love, it's called a pleasure...

When you add the desire to the love, it becomes your *prophet*.

Your prophet becomes your profit when you
do what you love and love what you do.
For it is said that "Your gift will make room for you"
Therefore, *never* give up on yourself or your dreams,
Even when things seem unclear, uncertain and unreal...
The sky is the limit and the only thing you have to fear is not trying.
My motto is and has always been "Anything is Possible"

Patricia

AuthorHouse™
1663 Liberty Drive
Bloomington, IN 47403
www.authorhouse.com
Phone: 1 (833) 262-8899

Because of the dynamic nature of the Internet, any web addresses or links contained in this book may have changed
since publication and may no longer be valid. The views expressed in this work are solely those of the author and do not
necessarily reflect the views of the publisher, and the publisher hereby disclaims any responsibility for them.

Any people depicted in stock imagery provided by Getty Images are models,
and such images are being used for illustrative purposes only.
Certain stock imagery © Getty Images.

This book is printed on acid-free paper.

ISBN: 978-1-6655-0053-1 (sc)
ISBN: 978-1-6655-0052-4 (e)

Library of Congress Control Number: 2020918195

Print information available on the last page.

Published by AuthorHouse 10/09/2020

authorHOUSE®

Printed in the United States
By Bookmasters